WHAT is in your HANDS can give you MILLIONS

GRACE J. MBONG

Library of Congress Control Number: 2012914270

ISBN: Softcover   978-1-4771-5613-1
        Ebook   978-1-4771-5614-8

Print information available on the last page

Rev. date: 11/06/2019

To order additional copies of this book, contact:
Xlibris
1-888-795-4274
www.Xlibris.com
Orders@Xlibris.com

Dedication

In Memory of my Father. Mr Mbong Johnny Mbong.

A Star Is Gone

A man of peace
Full of ambition, boldness and courage
Fear is not in his vocabulary because he stands strong at all times
The lord is my shepherd whom shall i fear
The lord is the stronghold of my life of whom shall I be afraid (Psalm 27 verse 1) Holy Bible.

He talks less and shows action for he believes that action speaks louder than words
He is a man that does a knee mark before a landmark
Always putting God in all things
That is who my father is.

Boasting and Pride is not his style
He is a gentle man full of grace
Always giving of himself to help others
Never asking for anything in return.

Thank you for everything you have done for me
I will always honor you Daddy and cherish you
Although you are gone, your legacy will always be remembered.
Farewell Daddy. You are a man after God's heart
Mr. Mbong Johnny Mbong.

Acknowledgements

I express my profound gratitude to God Almighty.
Thank you for the talents you have given me.

To my mother Mrs Grace K. Mbong.
Thank you for teaching me about what matters most and believing in me.
I love you.

My Siblings: Emmanuel and Joy Mbong.
You know me the best and have supported me in all my endeavors.
Thank you so much.

My Immediate family: Lilian Mbong, Steven Abunike.
Thank you so much for your love.

My friends: Masime Lwabanji, Ubong Willie Etuk, Mr. & Mrs. Omolara Rufai,
Mr. & Mrs. Osman Sesay, Alabaster Choir (Highest Praise Church of God),
Clearance Cesar and Eagles Chapel Ministry,
Thank you so much for your all your encouragements.

My Mentors: Pastor Emmanuel, Pastor Rapheal Grant,
Pastor Tony and Sherry Stallings.
Thank you so much for your godly wisdom and unique insights.

Contents

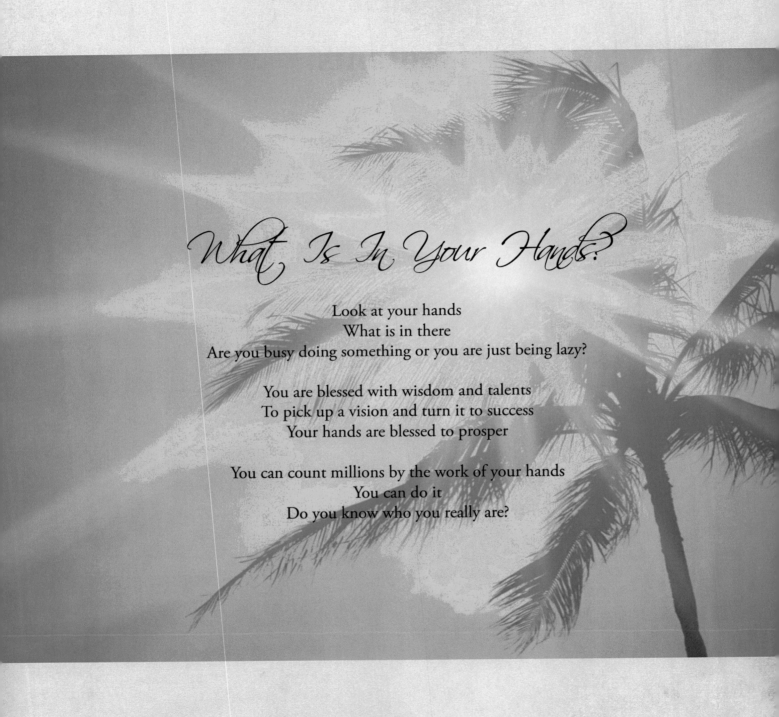

What Is In Your Hands?

Look at your hands
What is in there
Are you busy doing something or you are just being lazy?

You are blessed with wisdom and talents
To pick up a vision and turn it to success
Your hands are blessed to prosper

You can count millions by the work of your hands
You can do it
Do you know who you really are?

Are You Willing To Succeed?

Opportunities are all around you
You are blessed with strategies to succeed
Goals that have to come to be birth in life
Freedom to do whatever you want
Without restraints from any one because you are free

You have different resources that will lead to success
Are you willing to succeed?
In doing so, you will find fulfillment
If you are willing to strive and go for your dream.
Get up and push

Are you willing to take a take a step of faith?
Success is not easy, you have to work on it every day
Though sometimes you try and nothing works immediately
Don't give up on your dreams
Remember out of difficulties, grow miracles.

Stop Looking Behind

Stop looking behind
There is nothing behind for you
Stop dreaming about the past
Look ahead and think about the future

Yesterday is gone and is never coming back
You cannot change what happened yesterday
You have a bright future ahead of you
Focus on tomorrow.

Depend On God

When people walk away
You are left in the cold
Stripped and left for dead
Without no comfort

Tears roll down your face
Depression comes along to discourage you
What can you do in this critical time?
You must trust and depend on God

Obedience

How often do you obey God?
Do you listen, turn the other ear and act as if you are deaf?
People may laugh at you and mock at you but whose report do you believe?
The report of God or the report of man?

Why do you belittle the hand of God?
The hand of God is so powerful that it can turn things around for you
Do not turn to the left or to the right
There is no solution else where
If you obey God
You will live and prosper
God will prolong your days in the land where you possess
No man will be able to stand against you
(Deuteronomy 11 verse 25)

God will bless you as he had promised
You will lend to many nations but will borrow from none
(Deutronomy 15 verse 6) Holy Bible

Obedience is better than sacrifice.

Graven Idols

We all have things we worship and adore more than God
Is it money, jewelry, relationships, fame or luxury?
We cling to all of these things and spend quality time with them
We desire these things and neglect the purpose and the call of God for our lives
At the end of the day, everything is meaningless

Why do you push God to the curve?
Do you know that God is the one that gave you life?
God is your creator.
He needs your worship.

You shall not make for yourself an idol in the form of anything
In heaven and on earth, beneath or in the waters below
You shall not bow down to worship them
For I am a jealous God says The Lord God Almighty.
(Deuteronomy 5 verse 8-9) HolyBible

If you disobey God,
The Lord's anger will be on you
Worship God with all your heart
Let the graven idols go for it can't help you.
(Deuteronomy 6 verse 14) HolyBible

Will I Excel?

Will I succeed in whatever I do?
Yes you can
You don't need to end your life
Because of the things that have gone wrong.

You are not a failure. Failure is not in your blood line
You are born to win.
You are the head and not the tail.
God loves you my friend and he will never let you down.

Focus On Tomorrow

I was once in a desert
Wandering without no success
Walking from place to place
Having no place to go

Loneliness was all around me
No future, destination for my life
Sorrow and shame covered my face
For there was no one to show me the way.

Along the way, I heard a voice saying
Be strong and of good courage
For the Lord your God is with you
Is there anything too hard for God?

God can help you for no one will
He will provide for you when there is no way out
His name is called Jehovah Jireh my provider
Cast your cares on him for he cares for you

Yesterday is gone and it is never coming back
Let the hurts go and move on in life
You can't turn back the clock of yesterday
Focus on tomorrow and your future.

God Loves You

Who sits by your side in your darkest hour?
Who gives you inner peace when there is no one to help you?
Who makes a way when there is no way for you?
What satisfies you in your lonely moments in life?

Man might try to show you love but God's love is the best
Man may love you with condition but God's love is unconditional
God's love is true and God never disappoints
God loves you.

Make It Happen

You can choose to excel if you want to
You can also choose to be a failure
The choice is yours. This is all up to you
What are you doing with your life?

Stop giving excuses
Excuses is just a hole you dig and remain there
No one can help you in this matter
Get up, help yourself to attain success.

Success cannot be given to you on a silver plate
You must rise up and go for what you want
Remember go for your dream
Make it happen. Think about yourself.

God's Timing

Rushing without direction leads to failure
God knows the perfect time even though it looks illogical to us
His ways are not our ways neither his time tables are our own timetables
Wait on God for God's time is the best.

Energy

Energy is the capability of work or vigorous activity
What do you use your energy for?
Fear or Faith?

Change the language of Fear and embrace Faith
God has not given you the spirit of fear but the spirit of boldness and a sound mind
In times of trouble, do not fear.

The lord is my light and salvation whom shall i fear?
The lord is the stronghold of my life of whom shall I be afraid?
(Psalm 27 verse 1) Holy Bible.

Bloodline

What is in your bloodline?
You have the blood of a winner in running through your veins
You have the crown of royalty on your head
In your DNA, you are born to be successful
You are a champion that is who you are.

There Is A Baby In You

Every one of us have a baby buried inside of us
That cries for attention all the time
What are you doing with the gifts inside of you?

Your baby needs to come out so as to break forth for its mission
The talents and gifts needs nourishments
For the fire in you has to be activated.

You Cannot Survive Without God

Problems come along our way every day
We look for answers but there is no solution
God has the answer to all solutions.

Don't take your eyes off God
When all things fail, God never fails
Without God, you can't survive.

Who Are You?

You are a carrier of great destiny
Blessed by God for a purpose
Filled with great talents and wisdom
To succeed a better tomorrow
You are a child of God

Count Your Blessings

Life is filled with ups and down
That sometimes leads to doubts and fear
We go around in circles taking things for granted
Complaining and murmuring at all times in every situation we find ourselves

There are people who have lost their mind and sanity
People who are in worst shape than you think you are
Problems will come around but don't be discouraged
Trust in God and leave it there

Instead of complaining, begin praising God
Count your blessings and remember what God has done
You would not have made it this far if God did not show up
Never take this for granted.

Favor

You are strong like a lion
Favor is all around you
You are full of strength
Equipped to handle the task
For such a time like this

Favor is knocking at your door
Your brain is equipped for success
You can spread your wings like an eagle
For there is nothing that can stop you.

Trust In God

Take your eyes off man. Man cannot help you
Put your trust in God at all times
God will never leave you nor forsake you
For God is the source of life.

God Deserves The Credit

If not for God by your side, where would have you been by now?
Give all glory to God and don't ever think it's by your own strength
God deserves the credit and not you.

Choice

You can become anything in life if you want to
You can climb higher in success for the sky is your limit
If you are determined, it is possible
The choice is yours for the power is in your hands.

Doubt

Things happen at sometimes we begin to wander and doubt
Is God really real or is this a joke
We feel like letting go instead of holding on to God
Murmuring and saying to ourselves negative words

Don't doubt the word of God
The word of God is true and real
Believe in the word of God
For everything is possible to those that believe in the word of God.

Rejoice At All Times

Dont wait until everything looks good before you begin to praise God.
Thank God in good times and in bad times
Thank God when you are in the fire
You will never get out of the storm until you begin praising
The only weapon you have is Prayers and Praise

Bloom

Bloom where you are
God has placed you there for a reason
Expand your horizon
You can make it if you really want to in life

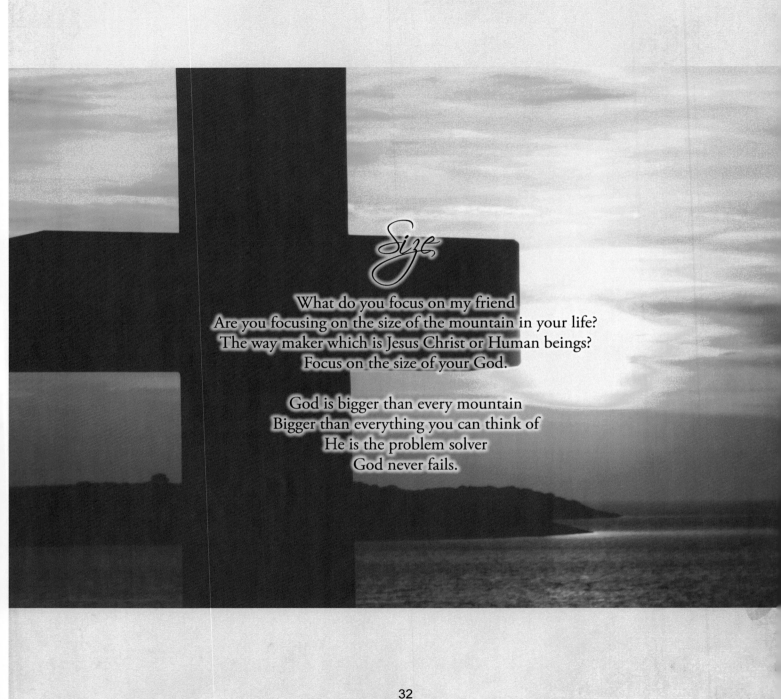

Size

What do you focus on my friend
Are you focusing on the size of the mountain in your life?
The way maker which is Jesus Christ or Human beings?
Focus on the size of your God.

God is bigger than every mountain
Bigger than everything you can think of
He is the problem solver
God never fails.

Wait

You cannot go ahead of God
If you do, you will fail
You are blind and you cannot see
Let God direct your path my friend

You may feel that waiting is only the waste of time
It is not necessary because I want my breakthrough now
My time is ticking, I have to go
If God directs your path, you will surely succeed

Remember They that wait upon the lord shall renew their strength
They shall mount up like eagles
They shall run and not be weary
They shall walk and not faint
(Isaiah 40 verse 3) Holy Bible

Seeds

Are you sowing good seeds or are you sowing bad seeds?
What are you planting in the ground every day of your life?
Seeds can grow and seeds can die
Do not be deceived. God cannot be mocked.
Whatever you sow, you shall reap.
(Galatians 6 verse 7) Holy Bible